My Dialogue with Death

My Dialogue with Death

ERNST E. KLEIN

Judson Press ® Valley Forge

My Dialogue with Death

Copyright © 1980
Judson Press, Valley Forge, PA 19481

Unless otherwise indicated, Bible quotations in this volume are from the Revised Standard Version of the Bible, copyrighted 1946, 1952, 1971, 1973 by the Division of Christian Education of the National Council of the Churches of Christ in the United States of America, and are used by permission.

Library of Congress Cataloging in Publication Data

Klein, Ernst, 1916-1979
  My dialogue with death.

  1. Spiritual life—Poetry. 2. Brain—Tumor—Poetry.
I. Title.
PS3561.L346M9   811'.5'4   79-26381
ISBN 0-8170-0867-5

The name JUDSON PRESS is registered as a trademark in the U.S. Patent Office.
Printed in the U.S.A. ⊕

CONTENTS

INTRODUCTION: A Maverick Ministry

With that self-understanding born of experience honestly examined, Ernst Klein came to accept his calling to a maverick ministry. In significant ways, even the definition of the term seems to confirm that description, "a recalcitrant individual who bolts his party or group and initiates an independent course."

That independent course often characterized his response to the situations of his life. It was in his theological thinking, often expressed in poetic images. It was also in his day-by-day ministry to congregations and college campuses. It became most manifest in his ministry at Old Cambridge Baptist Church just off Harvard Square during the tumultuous days of the sixties, where he courageously defended those who were in protest, even offering them sanctuary when others turned aside. For this he inevitably earned the respect of some, the opposition of others.

Yet his independence was of a particular nature. It was always *toward center* of the Christian gospel. That seemed the characteristic response of his ministry. Ernst Klein was not "far out." He was "far in," nearer center than many were willing to go. Not everyone has been able to see the distinction!

In the closing days of 1978 a new and unexpected challenge faced Ernst. In a matter of days a whole new and dominant factor came into his life when he discovered that he had a brain tumor and would need to be under treatment at the Massachusetts General Hospital for a period of weeks.

How did a maverick minister meet *this* basic human experience? Where did he find the certainties when the future was uncertain? These pages are the answer to that question. In a way consistent with his whole life, Ernst Klein met this time in his life with valor, sometimes touched with defiance, sometimes seasoned with humor, sometimes blunt in its honesty, but always with characteristic response—the move toward center. This response released in him a period of prolific and penetrating writing. Those writings are on these pages.

His ministry was diverse, even when marked by independence. After his graduation from Colgate Rochester Divinity School in 1940 he served pastorates in North and South Dakota, at Sawyer and

Brookings. In 1953 he went to the University of Kansas, where he was associate professor at the School of Religion and minister to about five hundred students at the Baptist Student Center. In recognition of his gifts in this area of ministry, he received a Danforth Grant and spent a year of special study at Boston University, 1957-1958.

It was in 1959 that he succeeded Dr. Samuel Miller as pastor of Old Cambridge Baptist Church, a ministry that was to continue until 1974. From 1974 to 1978 he was minister-coordinator for the Massachusetts Commission for United Ministries in Higher Education. In 1978 he began an interim ministry as executive of the Department of Church and Society of the American Baptist Churches of Massachusetts. On October 18, 1979, Ernst Klein died because of the debilitating effects of the brain tumor.

I am grateful to have known Ernst Klein through all these years and have counted him a warm personal friend. Our association has reminded me of a word from Macbeth, "He was a gentleman on whom I built an absolute trust." In his response to his illness, reflected so eloquently and movingly in these pages, Ernst Klein brought his independence of spirit to its finest expression. These words will endure to bear witness to us all in those times when demand upon us is absolute. Here is the faith of which Luther often spoke, "that faith which throws itself upon God in life or in death—this alone makes a Christian man."

Gene Bartlett

NOTE TO MYSELF

To be given "X" amount
of Time
before the surgeon
proceeds to cut and
drill and saw my
cranium
in pursuit
of the problematic
tumor which
may or may not be
benign and may
or may not be
embedded in my
brain and
entangled in my
cerebral blood
vessels—

to be given "X" quantity
of Time to recover
after scalpel and forceps
have done their work—

To be given Time
in any quantity
is suddenly recognized
as the gift
ineffable—

Time enough for
one more Christmas
with Clara and Jan and Jim and Debbie and
Krishan and all the rest so far and yet so near—

To be given time
to think about Time

and Timelessness and the
Great Beyond
from which all
real gifts come,
Thinking about all that,
Christmas '78 is
going to be
just GREAT!

P.S. It was!

E K

12/22/78

A NOTE TO FAMILY AND FRIENDS
Christmas, 1978

Time was, not long ago,
when time, apparently, didn't matter
                    all that much—
(if you missed one train, there was another, etc.)
Now, to me it is indubitably clear
                    that *time* IS *matter:*

But for the grace of Christmas . . .
("We can admit him to MGH* tonight,"
the good doctor said yesterday. "No
thanks!" said Jan, "we will have Christmas first.")

But for the grace of Christmas,
I would now be readied for the angiogram,
another brain scan, CAT* scan
(already I have seen one set of pictures!),
and then the good surgeon with knife,
drill, and saw will make a hole
above my right ear to remove
the madder matter, which has
produced these untimely symptoms
of senility (which friends say
they haven't noticed, but clear-eyed
Clara saw at breakfast last *Wednesday-Thursday*
and Jan said deserved immediate attention).
So by and *for* the grace of Christmas we are
together in our cozy Maine harbor: youngest
daughter Janet and friend Stephen,
strong son James with lovely wife Debbie
and charming two-year-old son Krishan,
and so many of you calling in
on Bell's wire to assure us of your love
and prayers.

*MGH—Massachusetts General Hospital
CAT—Computerized Axial Tomography

In recent conversations with the
Almighty, I reminded the All-Wise of certain
projects that await my efforts: a stone wall
to keep the sand dune off the backyard
(and the garage up), flowers to plant, high-
bush cranberries to see through their first
year here, together with six hybrid blueberries;
the Sam Miller project, the OCBC* story (tenta-
tively, "The Face of My Parish") and, of course,
walks on the beach with Clara, photography,
silk screens, stained glass to do. . . .

I'm sure the All-Knowing One has seen more
impressive agendas if not hubris!

Nevertheless, I have an omen:
This morning, about 5 A.M., that
bright planet Venus
shone through my window:

> "Alas for him who never sees
>   the stars shine through his cypress trees!"

Ours are only scraggly pitch pines,
but the star was very bright!

> "The light shines in darkness
>   and the darkness is not able to put it out!"

Ah, the grace of Christmas!
That holy mystery of the divine
love incarnate coming near
with healing touch and palpable joy
to all who will receive. . . .

Never did I so believe and see
that love from you-all touch
my innermost heart and hurt. . . .

*OCBC—Old Cambridge Baptist Church.

Where terror stalked in darkness
unchallenged, I now go unafraid
into that dark hour
trusting I will see and hear and
hold you all again, my friends.

Immer,

E K

12/22/78

DEATH

You old villain,
I see you smirking
behind the pleasant faces
of the nurses, the neurologist's
tricks, the surgeon's calculated
whens and wheres and what-ifs. . . .

I knew you were coming,
but I didn't expect you so soon. . . .

You say this is only your get-
acquainted visit; you're not here
on business? No matter! You
are what you are and I've seen your
work through the years. We've had
our brief encounters over other
people's bodies, but now your
sly smile and wink leave no doubt
of your intentions: I get it!
But don't be in such a hurry—
Surely your services are needed
elsewhere while I tidy up my affairs
a bit. Clara would appreciate that. . . .
Even more, I would like to sort out all those papers
I saved from 335* and put together my
Nevelson wall—You know I've saved
Some delicious junk. . . . And I need to learn
to use that router. . . .

I suppose that's what they all say—
Time, times, and half a time—
and *then* it's your turn—

*335 Harvard St. was the home of the Baptist
University Pastor in Cambridge, Massachusetts,
where the Kleins lived from 1959 to 1979.

Grin, you devil, I'll see you
on the other side where our powers
will be equalized and I'll have the
true perspective on your activities,
and mine.

Could we get together for a long talk
sometime—any time will do—
Maybe you can convince me of the
ultimate beneficence of your work
and maybe there will remain a nugget
or two among my foolishness that
someone will cherish.

E K

12/25/78

ALTERNATIVES

"Tomorrow," the good doctor
said. "Tomorrow morning,
we'll take you to the O.R.,
give you a local anesthetic,
and make a little burr hole
in your cranium—just
above your hairline on
the right. I'll do that.
Then at 2 P.M. we'll take
you to the X-ray room for the needle biopsy.
Dr. Zervice says your
case is ideal for that.
With this tinker-toy-like
contraption, and with X-rays
to see by, we'll guide the
needle to the trouble spot
and try to remove a bit
of tissue. Then soon we'll
know its nature. If it is an
abscess, we'll try to remove it
all. If not, chemotherapy or
radiation-therapy may be indicated.
Or we could go in later and
try to remove it. . . ."

Tomorrow—already the
sun is low. Unlike
yesterday, which dragged with
nothingness, today is far
gone. Tomorrow is almost
here. One more shave, one more
breakfast, one more sunrise,
then the Grim alternatives—
success or failure, life or
death or dimming half-life

for one who loved life so—
the odds are long in my favor,
but in the shadow of
good intentions and splendid techniques
lurks the Negative—the
unintended result—the
Black Omnipresence whose
shadow I have felt, whose breath comes
closer, whose name is
Death—
Who is also a servant of
the Almighty, for without
death there were no individuation,
no people, only continuous
vegetation. So now,
Soon, my turn comes. . . .
I deny it not, I
flinch not from the blow,
I go when called into that vaster world
whose harmonies we have
known here.

Hallelujah!

E K

1/3/79

PRAYER

Lord, now in the hour
  of my fear and doubt
  in the aloneness of my
  alone—make your morning star of
  hope shine once more
  in my heart.

Let my life praise
you yet many days in little ways
best known to you
and me.

LORD GOD of all
Sunrises, keep this
frail heart praising
YOUR GLORY.

                E K

            1/3/79

PATIENCE

The leaf miner excavates
the foliage of my young white birch,
turning the leaves brown in midsummer.

Inside the leaf this tiny pest is as
secure from my efforts at control
as from the chickadee or brown creeper.

Year after year I see the birch
leaves deformed, the evil tolerated
as nevertheless the tree grows
taller. Some things you
carry with you and, gradually,
outlast. . . .

E K

1/3/79

BETWEEN WORLDS

The beach
is a boundary
between worlds—

few cross the frontier
and live

a child picks up
pretty shells

E K

1/4/79

"POST-OP" NOTE TO GOD

Lord, here I am again, bounced
    back from the Abyss—
by pure grace
       out of the weakness of my strength
       out of the ignorance of my wisdom,
       out of the hopelessness of my hope—
Here "ex nihilo" I see, hear, walk, talk,
                and taste *again.*

And all my friends are glad
    I am to walk the earth again
    and do my special tricks.
You must be glad, too, because
    without you the good medics
    and all their fancy machines would be
              helpless.

So here we are, you and I, again
    to greet the dawn and Venus.
    and all your other creatures
      great and small.

      E K

      1/5/79

A PROBE TO THE HEART

"It is the not knowing what
the next trap will produce
that lends spice to the daily
gamble."—Lew Dietz, writing
        of the Maine lobsterman

That's it! The *not knowing*—
which means not being in control—
Not able to say "Next week, or
next month, next year I'll do thus and so."
"This project can be put off. . . ."
"I won't read this book now—after all,
I have it on the shelf: I can read it
        anytime!!!"
Anytime, you suddenly realize, for you, may
        never come. . . .
Now, you with the trembling lip,
You who saw strokes and other death
dealers always happening to someone else,
Now, your turn has come
to realize that you didn't invent yourself.
You, too, are mortal, and circumstances
beyond your control have intervened. . . .
You now have the great Enlightenment!
You who comforted others, now reach
        out for comfort. . . .

You, who preached faith, how now do you
        ground your life, your hope, your tomorrow?
The words you know so well; what
        substance do they have in your hour of need?

You, who were so self-sufficient,
        now You are helped to the bathroom.
You are doubly escorted on your wobbly
        walk down the hall. . . .

You, with the ready wit,
    your critique of every profession,
    now wait for every word from
    the doctor's lips.

You, with your plans for
    twenty years, will you get two?

You, with your own scheme for the
    denial of death (work, achievement),
    will you take it with you
    unfinished to the grave?

You, with pride in your powers,
    prepare to lay them down—

You, dear heart, so full of *hubris,*
    receive now the love showered
    upon you.

You, the consummate loner,
    feel the spirits hovering
    about you—people
    you have known and loved,
    as their prayers ascend
    to the great Giver
    who now calls you to account.
You, who so often pronounced the Shalom,
    now go in peace.

E K

1/7/79

one must say "yes"
to DEATH
otherwise it
simply
returns
  returns
   returns. . . .

E K

1/7/79

THE GREAT DENIAL

We all practice the denial of death
    pushing our knowledge
    that we are mortal
    at every tolling of the bell
    deeper into the subconscious
    and pretending to go about our business
    as if we knew nothing of Death. . . .

The strategy is faulty!
The enemy too strong!
The revelation of our true condition
    is inevitable.
It may be a sunny day or rain.
There may or may not be a messenger of pain.
Your work may or may not be done—
You may be planning a party on the beach
Or a great public extravaganza.
No matter!
The messenger will find you
The message unmistakably
    for you!

Then will all your strength
    of spirit be called upon
    to face this untimely,
    unwelcome Intruder.
And you do battle valiantly
Knowing eventually you lose—
The Great Necessity
    includes you—
There are no exceptions!

For this occasion some tribes
    have a death song.
Others speak of "a good death"
    meaning, I suppose, being
    prepared in every way
    and going gladly into that
    Great Beyond.

E K

1/7/79

TAKE CARE OF YOURSELF, WORLD

Take care of yourself, world:
I'll be checking out, soon.

Take care of
your hungry, your poor,
your teeming multitudes yearning to be free—

Take care of
full belly child saying
to empty belly child, "Look
at the pretty rainbow!"

Take care of
your crackpot politicians
your media preachers making a fast buck
and other schemers and dreamers
working for #1.

Take care of Indians
and immigrants
and refugees.

And please, take care
of wide-eyed children
who want to know the truth
about a world
where every prospect pleases
and only man is vile.

Take care of Dan, Krishan,
Jennifer, Mark, and Melanie . . . and millions more.
Please, Lord!
Take care of yourself, world!

> *E K*
>
> *1/7/79*

TOMORROW

"Tomorrow"

How often I have said that word
     as I put aside a task—
Now it is said to me in accents
     I cannot ignore.

Tomorrow, the O.R. will be ready
     for you—
Tomorrow good medics take up
     their best techniques against
     the evil matter in your brain.

Tomorrow the long shot is decided,
     as tissue becomes issue
     and life goes this way or
     that.
Tomorrow, I do not decide,
     I do not operate,
     I do not do good or bad—
except the prior decision of relinquishment.

Tomorrow I rest my case
     not knowing who or what
     will decide.
Tomorrow I accept the outcome,
     the verdict, the sentence . . .
Will it be life as I have known it?
No! Never again! Never will I live casually
     carelessly the sacred moments of the gift
                                        ineffable.

"On the border of the finite,"
     said Tillich, "one becomes aware
     of the infinite." Well said, Paulus!

On the edge of tomorrow, I
    remember yesterday's ecstasies,
    not least the morning star
    shining in my window. . . .
Surely the great Giver of all our good
    was tipping his hand there . . . and
    I'll be greeting many a dawn
    down East and beyond.
Come, my friends, the dawn is breaking.

E K

1/31/79

TIMELESS in OCEAN PARK

I have no time, not any
    nor do I want any
For time is a human abstraction
    imposed on the heavens and earth.
I've seen that time trap called Stonehenge
And the great clock at Salisbury Cathedral
I'd rather see a sunrise over Saco Bay!
And starlings huddle on the sunny side of a roof,
    A stray cat soak up the sun's rays
        Against the winter cold.
And sunrises! Give me thousands of sunrises.
Moons: waxing, waning, quarter, full, and crescent,
    Give me ten thousand assorted
        rising slowly
        playing with the clouds.
And Venus as the morning star!
    Wake me, early, but don't
    tell me it's five o'clock
The Big Dipper!
    Fill mine with strawberries
        so I can share with Dan!
And the North Star—keep it shining—
Give me these,
    but tell me not of time!
It's the phenomena we live by,
    not the abstractions!
Back of our glib words and ancient symbols
    is the primal event, the essential
    elemental episode by which we live:
Let there be light!
And it was so!

E K

1/6/79

LIFE as POSSIBILITIES

Life gets "iffier" with an
    extra hole in your head!
"There are no guarantees," the doctor
    said when I asked him
    about the efficacy of
    chemotherapy and radiology.

No guarantees! Were there ever any?
Why do we try to insist on
            perfect security?
Would I want an agreed
number of days and nights
to putter about concerns
considerably less than
cosmic in scope and significance?
No guarantee!
Did the Almighty have
guarantees when He/She/It,
    invented protoplasm
    box turtles
    humming birds
    Homo sapiens
    and free will?
Someone took a chance
turning us all loose here
    together. . . .
Where is it written that
    because there is sex
        there will be love?
    because there is power
        there will be justice?
    because there is one blood
        there will be community?
Someone took a long chance
    setting myriad possibilities
        in motion.

Without guarantees. . . .
So now, I affirm that arrangement.
No guarantees!
    One day, one hour at a time.
Thank you, Lord, for possibilities
    and help the technicians aim straight
    as they turn the radiation
        into my brain!

All we know of love
    and justice and community
is grounded in the general
    "iffiness" of things
Sparked by the Challenge
"I LIVE!"

                E K

            1/10/79

RELINQUISHMENT

How do you live with a tumor
    in the brain?
Gladly—if that's what you have!
And with heightened awareness
    of the precariousness of life—
We knew it all along—didn't we?

I had a biology professor once
    who had a definition of life.
    —a mysterious colloid of
    such and such properties—
    but from the way he lived
    his, I was not impressed!

Now that's the question, isn't it?
How to live the days (maybe years)
    that are left.
    How to pack each hour
    with joy.
    How to greet each dawn
        with surprised thankfulness.
    How to practice the fine
        art of relinquishment—
Taking only what we need,
and passing on our prized
possessions to those who
will appreciate them.

Then, finally, to return to the One
who gave it the spirit that has moved
in this decrepit hulk.

But wait, my friends,
    more is required:
There must be celebrations—
    as indeed there have been!
Family times of pure and robust laughter,
Times when, with friends and strangers, too,
    we shared the great moments
    of birth and death
    and rites of passage in between.

E K

1/6/79

CELEBRATE, MY FRIENDS

Celebrate, my friends,
    when this my life, too,
    is complete and I will
    have exchanged "the ambiguity
    of existence" for that
    full view of the Maker
    "face to face."

And be not concerned
    to mark my grave—
    If I have loved and
    labored well, there will
    be marks on souls I
    have touched—
    a truer record, even
    with its pain,
    memorial enough for me.

E K

1/6/79

THE ULTIMATE ABSURDITY

The ultimate absurdity:
a tumor in the brain
I see it black and writhing
although it gives no pain—

No pain, did I say?
For this monstrosity I have
endured the work of the surgeons,
a score of infernal machines. . . .

But the pain it gives
is at the heart
where dwells my love of Maine
like walking on the beach
with Denmark Dan* again.

E K

1/12/79

* E K's Danish grandson.

THE COMPASS

The strong North Pole
attracts my compass.

The soul points straight to God.

E K

1/12/79

SOMEWHERE

Oh, heart, heart, heart,
do not break!
Somewhere this river of sadness
must end:
Somewhere Venus shines
Somewhere another dawn!

E K

1/12/79

LETTING GO

You know I never had much power, Lord,
So why do I find letting go so hard, so hard?
When I think of Clara there alone in Maine
No one to chop the kindling
Dig out the snow drifts
Keep an eye on the roof—
Is your computer jammed, Lord?
I thought you were doing better than this!
Or is it all a game of chance?
Did all those prayers never find their way?
Are you a cruel trickster, Lord,
Letting us work for forty years
And dream of quiet beside the beach
And now to come to this?
I know, I know, we have not seen the end—
Nor all the circumstances you must count—
But right now it looks rough,
Lord, very rough ahead—
And *worst* of all is not to know—
That's not our part, you say?
You say our part is trust?
I've had so little practice at that, Lord,
Could you give me a few more lessons?

E K

1/12/79

THE SO-CALLED "LIFE SHELL"

The so-called "Life Shell"
is more elegant than a snail
somewhat less majestic than the chambered nautilus. . . .
It has an elegance of shape and texture all its own.
(Could the Almighty create anything ugly if He tried?
Maybe we deal with a finite Deity after all!)

I hold you in my hand, little life shell
wondering where you came from.
How long did it take you to secrete this
lovely souvenir of a life?
How long did you hide here from unnumbered
enemies in the Great Deep, furtively reaching
out to prey on lesser creatures for sustenance?
Whatever the answers, I'm so glad that you lived and have
now come to me!
I live near the ocean, often walk the beach
winter and summer, looking at daily deposits
from the Great Chain of Life along the high tide mark.
Never have I seen your like—only distant relatives,
each with its own charm.

What is the meaning of this gift?
It came to me in my near-fatal trauma:
The intention, I think, was that I should
think of life, not death, hope and not despair.
This you have helped me do. But more than
that to think of life *and* death and then again life!
That is how it is for you, now handsomely
displayed in a brass crescent stand at my bedside.
Before that you were a cherished item of commerce
in the Shell Gallery in Newton Centre.
Tell me, precious one, is this heaven for you?
At the very least you have a second life!

And if you, dare I doubt it shall be so for me?
Even though I never learned to secrete
a shell (though some thought me a crusty hard-shelled
type), I think I have grown a soul!
Would you know about that? Do
crustaceans have souls? I suppose it
possible, since all creatures have relationships
and it is in interactions with one's fellows
and with the Almighty that the soul is born and grows.
I was fortunate to have been loved and cherished
from birth and taught to love others and above all
the Good Lord Above. This I have tried to do,
with uneven success through the years.
A sense of God's presence became "second nature"
to me. Once on our ranch in Montana, Father
was away for weeks (he was an area evangelist and pastor)
and Mother had to go to the neighbor's (two miles away).
When she told my sisters and me that we would be alone
for awhile, I objected, "No, God will be right here with us!"
I guess I was about four years old. How can one get
over "conditioning" like that? Public schools, street
gangs, a "godless" state university, and even a so-
called liberal seminary didn't phase it. (I even
lived in dorms!) One year at the U. we had a little
food co-op in the biology department! First time I
used Mazola, mayonnaise instead of butter (and on
desperate days, we liberated cheese from the experi-
mental rats)! How else do you stay alive on $17.50 a
month? And then the good State of North Dakota in-
sisted I should pay property taxes before collecting
my last check! So I got on the rolls. Years later,
in seminary, I got a letter from the sheriff saying
if I did not pay promptly, he would have to come
after it! Ah, yes, the great struggle for survival
occurs on land and among Homo sapiens as well as in
the sea! But I digress: I was speaking of souls.
I have never maintained a spiritual discipline,
except as a part of my profession—working hard
and taking every opportunity for growth.

What makes me think I may have grown a soul
is this sudden, unexpected, overwhelming, outpouring
of love from so many people near and far—
many of whom I have known only slightly.
All insist I have influenced them for good.
Today I received a letter from a student I have
never met: She has a hearsay acquaintance.
It was a beautiful letter. She has the heart
of a pastor!

So now the mystery changes!
The question now is not, why did this
happen to me? Why now, in the
face of our beautiful plans for retirement?

The question now is, what did I do
to deserve or even to inspire such love?
And how can I ever repay it?

I've pretty well decided I'm not going to die,
Soon that is. But, of course, life will be so
different. One cannot face the ontological shock—
look Death and non-being in the face—
and remain the same!!

Now, I'm freed up as never before. As my old pal
Gus Hintz said after his near fatal heart attack, "Ernie,
now I'm no longer afraid! I can tell those _____ exactly
what I think!"
Not that I have scores to settle! Only obligation of love!
But I don't fear the future. I don't
come to a stammering halt at the thought
of death. Look, I've faced it! And you, Life Shell,
helped me do it. The Great Economist is a great
conservationist also.

>   E K

>   1/20/79

O BACTERIA

O bacteria: you single-celled wonders!
I remember you from my days as a biology major at good old U.N.D.
How I admired your mono-magnificence—then!
A tiny bit of protoplasm going it alone in this big bad world.
I worried a bit about you then, I really did!
Even knowing your propensity for galloping mitosis (cell division).
I thought you were beautiful—there on the slides under 600X.
I must say, with all due respect to fellow creatures, the
love affair is over—for good!
Now I cheer on your deadly enemy—the antibiotic and the penicillin.
Eagerly I take the pill that turns my urine (and my pj's) orange!
And I drink the sweet acid cranberry juice to flush you out of
my system—forever, I hope. You even gave me a fever, you
impudent little bastards (a well-considered word).
Did you have to humiliate me so?
Wasn't it enough that the cancer caused my early senility
(drooping lip, crying, unsteady hands and feet?)
Now you come along, billions strong, gang up on me and impose
upon me this messy infantilism—infantile-senility is what I've
got—thanks to you!
What did I ever do to you? Of course I did sterilize a few
hundred petrie dishes in the pressure cooker when I taught botany
lab (I kept thinking it would blow up—until the Home Ec. senior
kindly came to my rescue). Was it for that?
Are you a vengeful lot? Have you been tracking me for decades
from N.D. to S.D. to Kansas, then left to Harvard?
Or do you strike at random? (Would seem more befitting your
station in life!) Aha! Maybe that's it! You attack humans
for our arrogance and pride—just because we featherless bipeds
with pentadactyl appendages and a large brain think we're
the cream of creation, the apex of evolution, the master
species, we think we must dominate the earth, reshape it to suit
ourselves, and even reach out to the moon and the planets!
Everything must serve our every whim and fancy!
(I admit some of those fancies are pretty bad.
Have you seen any of our TV ads? or federal budgets?)

Actually I have opposed some of the more vulgar and
dangerous—atomic power and war. You may not have known
Dr. Schweitzer. Well, I'm with him on reverence for life!
You should see some of my Kodachromes of lichens and seaweed,
sand and sedges, and this year the rare cardinal flower!
Hope you don't mind if I brag a bit.
OK, you win round one! I am thoroughly humiliated—cut down to
size (well, not quite!). I remember Barry Commoner saying
"Nature bats last!" Is that what you're telling me now?
I know there's a lesson in this somewhere, having always had
the faith that whatever happens, something good will come of it
before God is through with it. Good for me or good for you?
Shall we flip or leave it to heaven? Well, my microscopic
ex-friends, I want you to know two things: (1) There will be no
ill will in that penicillin I'm about to take. I respect
your right to exist—especially when it's *not* at my expense
and embarrassment! God made you a part of his superabundance.
For the life of me I don't understand why He had to make two
     thousand
or more species of you (one would have done, it seems).
That alone cost me three extra days of the miseries, not to say
what it did to devoted Clara, my washerwoman wife and lover,
while we waited for the culture to be grown. (2) This encounter
should be quite enough between us! You know my resources for
resistance as I yours for attack! We've gotten acquainted.
Let's say, we've reached an understanding: *(a)* Enough is
enough! *(b)* Speaking of enough—if God made us, there is
enough and to spare for every living thing. By the way,
yesterday I saw twenty lusty crows cawing as they played
"King of the Castle" on the roof of Davis Hall and surround-
ing trees. (I don't think they know the rules!)
Ever eaten crow? I know some who have. . . .
Maybe you'd enjoy it!
On that recommendation (most sincere)
I bid you now farewell. *Auf Wiedersehen nimme!**

    E K

    1/22/79

*Schwäbisch for *never*

44

GOOD OUT OF EVIL?

When I was reminded that God turns evil into good, and that
"We know that in everything God works for good with those who
    love him,
who are called according to his purpose" (Romans 8:28), I could not
    conceive how
possibly this could apply to me—though I gave my intellectual
assent to the proposition. It simply had no concretion: I felt
utterly numb, helpless—no ground under my feet, the future
completely fogged in, all plans wiped out!

The only reality was the hospital routine: the drugs, the nurses,
MDs, CAT scans, the blood-letter, the urinal, four walls, an
empty ceiling, an unworkable TV, a radio with dead batteries, and
the knowledge I would be awakened repeatedly for "vital signs"
and pills, and by the clatter of the cleaning crew and the break-
fast trays.

Desperately I prayed, feeling my words bounce off that empty
ceiling! Now, only ten days later, with nine radiation treat-
ments, look what God hath wrought!! Could anyone have imagined
the creation? Or the resurrection? Slowly, I rise again!
My strength returns! My brain works!

My thoughts are of life, not death!
Life with new priorities, new joys!
A life of new accomplishments. Having faced
Death and spoken my heart to Him,
I am no longer afraid!
I know the Mightier One, the Life-
Giver, the freedom-bringer, the One
who calls me to live to the praise
of his glory!
This I intend to do!

E K

1/22/79

AM I GOING TO GET WELL, LORD?

You saw how steadily I walked
                    to the john.
You heard the doctor say "good," "good,"
"good" when he examined me on Thursday.
You know that tumor is shrinking.
We've been zapping it real good,
Lord, with your divine cobalt. . . .
The doctor said soon they'll take an
X-ray to see what is left.
Could I have just one little sign,
                    Lord?

You say these are the signs?
I did see a light through the curtains
just now, but I know it's only
                    the street light!
How about another glimpse of Venus?
You say it's not time for Venus to rise—
And besides, it's cloudy!
You understand, Lord, it would
be so nice to know, for sure, to be
                    able to plan. . . .
It's so hard living with question
marks after everything, with all
these uncertainties. . . .
Not only for me, it's hard on
the family, too, you know!

You say you prefer to deal with
possibilities and probabilities, not
      dead (oops) certainties?
You say it's more fun that way, Lord?
(Helps keep us humble down here on earth?)
Yes, Lord, I remember our previous
                    conversation!

E K

1/29/79

THANKS, ARCHIMEDES!

Without your principle,
I understand the flush toilet would have been impossible!
I want you to know I really have
appreciated your contribution during these miseries!
I tremble to think where we'd be without it.
I lived for years in ranch houses and
primitive parsonages with *no* running water.
(Correction: it ran when we ran, carrying it both ways!)
There always was more going out!
I've seen and used every known model of outdoor biffy,
one-holers to four-holers, some with trenches
in every kind of weather—from 110 in the shade to
40 below! Sometimes we had to dust off the snow with
the ubiquitous Sears Roebuck Catalogue!
And chamber pots! I've seen enough of them!
So, thanks, Archimedes! Millions, unknowingly
join me in this tribute!
My Aunt Martha, a real pioneer gal
turned evangelist via Moody Bible Institute
and now a confirmed urbanite, still
has a vendetta against all outdoor johns.
I heard her say once she would like to take
a plane and personally bomb every biffy
in both Dakotas. I want you to realize,
Archimedes, that she just might do it, too.
Could lose her life that way (accident or shot
down mistaken for a Commie). What a way to go!
I am sure Aunt Martha has considered those risks.
I am equally sure she is still determined!
So, on the alert, all primitive farmers
and ranchers in North and South Dakota! Scan your
horizons daily for a low-flying, erratic plane!

E K

1/23/79

HAIR

My hair is falling out!
By the handful!
I dare not comb it or it
will be all gone.
Might as well. . . .
Yesterday, at church,
they said I looked great!
Now, thinking of going out
for my treatment and to
that important meeting at 5,
I reach back for an old jingle:

    My face, I don't mind it,
    for I am behind it—
    It's the people in front
    that I jar. . . .

No! Let's not say that!
Let's say, "Look! This is
What answered prayer
looks like!" Amen!

      E K

      1/29/79

ON BEDSIDE MANNERS

A. *The Doctor*

I liked the head resident in neurology.
Always pleasant, he was gentle but firm
as he tested my reflexes and coordination,
with special attention to the left side. . . .
Best of all, he was, unlike my surgeons (one
to make the hole, one to go in!), available. . . .
Then, about the tenth day, I think it was,
he popped in with a jolly, "And how are you today?"
"That's my line," I said, showing my frustration.
"I haven't seen Dr. _____ and Dr. _____ since the
operation—or if I have, I can't seem to
get any information and especially any prognosis.
So, tell me, how am I, Doc?"
He looked me in the eye as I had never
seen him look at me before:
"If I were in your place," he said, "I would
get my affairs in order. . . . Who knows
what will happen in six months. . . ."
"O my God," I felt myself saying, though
I'm sure no words crossed my lips.
"And after all those prayers! O Hell!"
Now the Abyss was yawning wide . . . no
ground under me, no sky above, only
the great primordial VOID—NOTHING—
I began to fall down, down into nothingness,
too numb, body and soul, to resist. . . .
When I looked up, the good doctor was leaving.
"Thanks a lot, Doc!" I managed to get
out through my tears, in my inimitable
sarcastic style, "I needed that—like I
need another hole in my head."

B. The Nurse

Within a minute, or so it seemed, the
nurse was there. Seeing my condition,
she said, "Is anything the matter? Are you OK?"
"Yeah, I'm OK—I don't need anything. . . .
Except I just found out I may have six
months. . . ."
"Oh, that _____ _____ _____," she exploded,
"He never should have said that!"
"You mean it isn't true?" Desperately I
clutched for a straw, a root, a twig—
like a falling mountain climber in mid-air.
"It's not necessarily so," she said. "He had
no right to say it. . . . He doesn't know!
only God knows!"
"And He isn't telling," I said.
"That's the way it is. . . . but you must have faith!
Many people have remissions from the radiation. . . ."
Now she came over and sat on my bed.
"It's all right to cry . . . go ahead and cry."
And then,
     she took my hand!
Now I know what my poet son Jim
meant when he wrote about his
hospitalization for mental illness.
He said nurses were more helpful
than the doctors, and the orderlies, cleaning
ladies, and food people even more helpful
than the nurses. And the most helpful
were his fellow-patients. I think the
point is empathy, humility, and simply
being there with you with no conceits, no
professional pretensions, with only your
humanity, confessing your own needs. . . .
It's what Bonhoeffer calls the view from below!

C. The Clergy

There is a breed of "born-again" evangelical
positive thinkers who do not hesitate,
specifically and at length, to tell you
(and everyone else) *and* the Lord God Almighty
exactly what to do, as for example:
"Now, Ernie, there's no doubt about it
Whatsoever—just get that out of your mind—
You're going to get well. That's all there is to it.
I'm not talking about your surgery and your
radiation medicine or your chemo or whatever.
I'm talking about FAI-ITH. You know
what I'm talking about. Now there may be some
things about your theology not pleasing to the
Lord (he didn't say this, but I have always sensed
it in his attitude). Let's pray!!" (Not, would
you like me to pray with you?)
Grabbing my hand, he pressed
the button of his direct (one-way) line to the Lord:
"O God, you know our dear brother Klein—
You know his needs—you know all our needs.
And we know you will meet all our needs.
We know you will heal our brother Ernie.
Now give him faith, real faith, to put all
his trust in you, O God, and make him well real soon. . . .
OK, Lord, in the name of Jesus Christ
we pray, Amen!"
He looked at his watch. "Got another
patient here. Got to run. Here's our
church bulletin for next Sunday. You
are on our prayer list. Now, Ernie,
keep the faith. It's that simple! God bless."
And he was gone.
Twice in one week this happened.
The miracle is that the church survives!

* * *

My friend Lou popped in unexpectedly,
His jolly, round, beaming face like
a new moon, or the sun through clouds.
"How you doing, pal?"
We've been through some rough waters, Lou and I.
Together for almost twenty years, I could always
count on Lou. He had just come through
a major operation, kidney stones.
I asked him how he felt and he touched
his side, which was still tender.
It was Lou who said the secret of survival
in hospitals is simply, "Endure."
Today his message was different.
Apparently he had decided to challenge me,
and nothing in his perception of my condition
dissuaded him. Suddenly he reached 'for his
hat, then blurted out, "Ernie, it's really
very simple: All you've got to do is
believe what you've been preaching
all these years!" And he was gone!
Thanks a lot, Lou, old pal! Just
what I needed . . . to be reminded
of all those old sermons, those platitudes,
those copied illustrations, those questionable
interpretations of the Word,
those romantic perversions of the gospel—
Those prayers at funerals of little children,
those committal services at gravesides.
Thanks a lot, brother! Right now,
I have trouble believing anything
except my own dying—
and you want me to grab onto
that trash I was peddling. Lou,
if you only knew. . . .
Lou, Lou, don't go, don't go!
And don't say anything like that ever again.
Just let me see your moon face beaming—
But he was gone.

Then there was brother G, not saying
much beyond, "Is there *anything* I can
do?" And he'd sit there, make small talk
for three or four minutes. Then, "Would
you like me to say a prayer with you?"
I nodded and he took my hand.
I do not remember the words, but I
prayed with him, adding an Amen
to every sentence of thanksgiving, hope,
and trust. The ceiling cracked!
He was gone, but then I remembered
how he had come the day of the "procedure"
and kept vigil, with Walt (my minister) ready
to comfort Jan and Clara if things went wrong. . . .
You were there! Thanks, brothers Gene, and Walt, and John D.

D. The Laity

To a friend:
    You came
    when I thought I was as good as
            dead,
    And made me feel
            alive!

            E K
            1/31/79

PRAYERS UNDER RADIATION

I have three prayers with which to meet the lethal
                                        radiation.
You better believe I was scared (still am!).
For three nights I dreamt of that infernal machine.
For a week I worried about the competence
of technicians, the chances for error. . . .
My worst nightmare was that someone touched
the disintegrator button, and that was IT!
Fortunately there was also a re-integrator button
and finally someone found it, and here I am.

                    *****

On that black litter table, I feel like
a bit actor in a science fiction drama:*
The little red light sending rays down on my head
from a hole in the ceiling. My head taped down,
the talk about "center line," "angles," etc., the TV
monitor (technicians leave the room, operate
by remote control, and watch me on TV.)
Paradox: The killer heals, the healer kills!
Radiation causes cancer, radiation destroys cancer!
Death/Life: Out of the killer comes forth sweetness
With precise control, that is.
A sweet little bell sounds faintly. Then a soft
buzzing in the left answered by a harsh buzzing on the right.
Repeat twice. Hold. Change machine to other side.
Re-aim, retreat, fire!

                    *****

At first my prayer was the one I
learned from Grandma Keck at those

*Or like the sacrificial victim in a neo-Mayan cult!

55

tearful farewells after family reunions:
"Gott befohlen!" meaning "Committed to God"
or "In the hands of God!" That is, till we meet again.
It's like Dr. Arbuckle, the preacher in Newton Centre,
saying to the fundamentalists, "I can give you
my creed in eight little words: 'Father, into
thy hands I commend my spirit'"—which, of course,
is what Jesus said on the cross. What need for more?
I like the short version in Grandmother Keck's
German: "Gott befohlen!" I used it on my first
trans-Atlantic flight on Seaboard and Western.
I especially used it in Brookings when they revved
up the engines of the little hedgehopper
before taking off for Minneapolis. Scary!
Gott befohlen! This is a prayer that works,
at least for me!

Sometimes I pray spontaneously, in the vernacular.
I have heard that a positive attitude helps
conquer cancer. Suddenly I found myself
saying, "Sock it to 'em, Lord!" Get those
blankety-blank bad cells! Zap 'em, Lord!
And I guess that's what's happening!
This also "works"!

*****

Then came this letter from Mother, now eighty-five,
And she writes fondly of her only son, "You
were my preacher at age three. When it was getting
dark outside our house in Montana—
(a storm coming up?), you said, 'Look, the Heavenly
Father's lights are shining!'"

So now I have three prayers
(use in any order):

Gott befohlen/Father, into thy hands I commit my Spirit,

Zap 'em Lord! Sock et tu 'em!

(I visualize the writhing viper in my brain
perforated by a billion bullets moving
so fast they leave no hole in my cranium.)

Heavenly Father, let your light shine!
accelerate your divine atoms and electrons
to blow the smithereens out of that
evil cancer in my brain! Shine!
Shine! Shine on me, Heavenly Light!
(And God, please help them aim it straight!)
Shine, Heavenly Light! Hallelujah.
Amen!

I close my eyes, calm and relaxed.
Soon Mary and Jennifer come, gently
helping me down and back to the Reception,
Radiation Medicine, where Debbie and Pat
preside over the chaos of inpatients,
outpatients, doctors, technicians, nurses,
litters, volunteers, drivers, intercoms,
telephones, plus unforseen emergencies to keep
things from getting dull!

Another day, another treatment!
How many is that? Six! Only twenty-six more!
Five more weeks of scares and prayers!!
"Good-bye, Debbie, see you tomorrow!"
"Have a good day, Mr. Klein!"
"Thanks! You, too, Debbie."

E K

1/22/79

NAVIGATOR

Today I learned that I will never again
  drive a car!

The problem is the possibility of seizures,
  the probability of which, and time, and place
  are totally unpredictable. . . .
  But the possibility is always there,
  due to the altered nature of my brain.

Me never drive again! I've had a love affair
  with cars since that first forty-dollar
  Plymouth jalopy that I used to commute
  from Rochester (CRDS*) to the Batavia Friends
  Meeting. And then those Fords,
  that second-hand Olds, that dinosaur Frazer,
  the battered old Lincoln sport sedan—
  the faithful modest Dodge—

To freeze behind the wheel is not ideal—
  Besides, it would endanger others. . . .
  OK. I can live with that. No driving ever again!

Now Clara is the driver (her turn!).

I've told her I'm going to be one helluva navigator—
  back-seat driver, tire changer, maintenance person!
  And I'll have time to read, do the CB,
  watch the scenery, and take naps!
  Not a bad arrangement, though
  it might slow us down on long trips.

*Colgate Rochester Divinity School

St. Peter was not so fortunate.
   He was told by our Lord that he would
   be taken where he didn't want to go. . . .
   And he was!

At least I'm the navigator—for now!

   E K

   2/1/79

LESS IS MORE

You know, Lord, it seems to me
that I am getting more out of life these days
more than ever before—
    just when I was adjusting
    to the idea of expecting (demanding?)
    a great deal less!
Is this possible, Lord?

All these outpourings of affection and appreciation—
some from people I scarcely know—
I know this will taper off
    as I get back to my
    new "normal". . .
    As people realize I'm going to be around awhile,
    they'll save their flowers. . . .

I'm impressed, and so is Clara, by the
    new quality in our marriage—
    the mutual appreciation and support—
    How did you ever produce one like her, Lord?
    She is one of your masterpieces!
    (You say you don't make no junk, Lord? Amen!)

And then there's time; It's always seemed so scarce!
    Time to read and reflect
    Time to write (I never was much of a
    letter writer; now I have an extensive
    correspondence.)
    Time to sit at the window. Yesterday
    I saw this big flock of sparrows
    chirping in the apple tree with one big
    solitary silent crow. Somehow I know
    they were making plans for spring!

Is it possible, Lord?
    More for less?

You say less *is* more in your economy?
    Is that what Jesus meant when he said,
    "Blessed are the poor"?

Yes, Lord, less is more; Thank you, Lord!

E K

2/1/79

MOUNTAIN AND ABYSS

*To J B, who said she was finally getting to know me,   that I
wasn't hiding anymore, thanks!*

In his hand are the heights and the depths
You take the high road, and I'll take the low. . . .

*****

Martin Luther King, Jr.,
said he'd been to the mountain
just before he was shot by that human viper
in the stinking bathroom of the roominghouse
across from the motel.

Because he'd been to the mountain, Martin
could say, "I've seen the Promised Land—and it works!"
"Free at last! Thank God Almighty, I'm free at last!"

Brother Martin, I want you to know that
I'm still crying your dying. We need you
now. Without you, something vital has gone
out of the soul of America. We need you to
tell us the truth about America and the world,
about multinationals and starving children, about
Coca-Cola and conscience, about the compromises,
political expediency, and just plain vulgarity
in the new budget of our "born again" President. . . .
Without you, Martin, the soul of America is dumb.

I marched with you into Montgomery
and in Cambridge and on Boston Common.
I remember how you catalyzed and converted
thousands in Washington, D.C., jammed between
the monuments of Washington and Lincoln.
I was there. Afterwards, waiting to board
the bus for the all-night ride to Boston, a

woman I had never seen before begged me to trade
my bus ticket for her airplane ticket. You made
her feel guilty for having flown! You touched
her soul to make her trust an utter stranger.
You really turned her around. (Come back, Martin!
America needs a lot of turning around!) "Here's
the keys to my car," she said. "And here's
the parking ticket at Logan. I'd appreciate it
if you'd leave it at the station in Roxbury
where this bus will arrive." It was a deal!
I got home in time to see it all again on TV.
Just wanted you to know, Martin.

You've been to the Mountain.
I've been to the Abyss!
Never could get it all together like you did,
Martin. Never could find the words, the music,
the courage (or was it the life-style?) to say it
and make it stick!

Now I've been to the Abyss, over the edge!
Remember the one about how our Catholic friends
make holy water? They simply boil the Heck out of it!
Well, I've had the Hell scared out of me!

I got so scared I found myself thanking
        the nurses for waking me up at
        2 and 4 A.M. to take my vital signs
        and feed me pills. . . .
        I even thanked the bleeder for taking
        his innumerable samples!

I thanked the cleaning lady,
the food people (one to bring in the
menu card, another to pick it up,
still another to bring the passable
computerized food).

After twenty-one days I got so thankful for every

reminder that I was alive and might possibly
be alive tomorrow, that when I got out,
I found myself thanking Clara
for waking me up at 4 A.M. for my pills,
for making breakfast, doing laundry, typing,
driving, shopping—everything!
Repeatedly, spontaneously, I kissed her,
told her she was beautiful and that I love her!
Was I making up for lost time, or trying
to make points with the Almighty?
Anyway, I'm a changed man, Martin.
You don't look into the Abyss and come away
unchanged! Clara says she doesn't care if
I ever get back to normal!

A friend says she hopes a little of the
impishness remains, just so she'll recognize me.
Maybe she won't!
I'll never be the same:

    I've been to the Abyss!
    Free at last!
    Thank God Almighty,
    I'm free at last!

      E K

      2/2/79

REACHING

My "Pemaquid pines" are really
spruce, erect as soldiers around
the seaside boulder. Brought them
home in a number 10 can, I did,
six years ago.
Set them down in this sandy soil
and they've been happy ever since,
though in winter I see only the
bud-crowned tip of the tallest,
I know come spring they'll resume
their reaching for the stars.

E K

12/12/78

WARNING: PHOTOSYNTHESIS!

My copper beech will reach
to my ankles! But I see
the magnificent specimen, which
has stood more than a century
in Cambridge, from which
this seedling sprang. And I
see those precious cigar-shaped buds
enclosing the sacred ability to
transform the sun's energy into growth.
I stand back expectantly!

E K

12/28/78

DOWN EAST

We have this place Down East
where each day white gulls
patrol the pitch pines on
the edge of sand dunes
and our snug cottage
keeps a welcome hearth.
With timbers holding precious
loam, we have a corner of
perennials, a rose or two,
and berries to redden Clara's
homemade ice cream.

We've brought a precious store
of memories here, from far-away
Dakota days and Kansas and
Cambridge. Best of all,
we have each other, lives
we've shared since far-off Rochester,
Now enriched each day as
news comes from New Jersey, Muncie,
Boston, and Denmark.

Down East is a
cozy harbor.

E K

12/28/78

THREE GIFTS*

For Old Cambridge Baptist Church

Two gifts the Almighty gives to all,
A third gives them perfection:

Sunrise . . .
Sunset. . . .
and then the afterglow
into which all must go.

Two gifts we receive from the Almighty,
A third gives us perfection:

Sunrise . . .
Sunset. . . .
Then comes the afterglow
into which all must go.

Hallelujah! Hallelujah! Hallelujah!

Amen. Shalom forever. Amen!!

E K

2/1/79

*A hymn in the style of Proverbs 30.

WITH YOUR PERMISSION, LORD

With your permission, Lord,
I'd like to believe I'm going to get well!
Believe it as strongly as my tactless evangelistic
                                    friend,
As strongly as dear Lou who complimented
me with the challenge to believe
not knowing I was lower than low. . . .

You see, Lord, I've been reading this great book
by this good doctor in Texas
who helps cancer patients participate
in their recovery through proper attitudes,
emotions, and expectations, i.e., faith.

I am thoroughly convinced, Lord, that
this tumor was laid on me not by
chance, nor evil forces of Nature, nor
by the Devil, and certainly not by you, Lord.

I see very clearly that my own faithlessness,
my giving up on myself in certain
recent crises, my self-deprecation and refusal
to believe I had a meaningful future—
Forgive me, Lord! These were awful
errors that contributed directly to the
growth of the tumor by suppressing
my body's immunity system—
which you put there, Lord, when I
was so fearfully and wonderfully made.
Forgive me, O God!

Now with your permission, Lord,
I'd like to turn around, repent,
and be saved!
If I can participate in causing illness,
I can participate in the cure!

You know, Lord, how much
I was on your side on the side of life—
That is, until I became a burnt-out case!
Now accept me once again as one
of those who choose life, first of all
my own!

I know it is open-ended
and ultimately still in your hands
like the whole Creation.
You know what I mean, Lord!
I want to live—for life
and for you!

You say it's OK, Lord?
OK for me to have faith, to trust
to expect, to have confidence, to *plan?*
Hurray! (I've already begun
the exercises.) Already I can relax and sleep!
Already I'm sure I'm going to build
that stone wall in Maine—maybe even
Denmark for Christmas!

Thank you, Lord! Thank You, thank You!

E K

2/6/79

THE WILL OF GOD IN CHRIST

Rejoice always.
Pray constantly.
Give thanks in all circumstances;
for this is the will of God in Christ Jesus for you.

My pious mother, age eighty-five, laid that on me
in her last letter. "Ernie, read 1 Thessalonians 5:16-18
and take it to heart. It has helped me and
it will help you. God's Word is a lamp
unto my feet. . . ."

Rejoice always? Does that include
when the nurse can't find my vein for the
I.V.? When the bleeder wakes me at 2 A.M.?
When the doctor says "six months"? Ever
had an angiogram, Brother Paul?

In *all* circumstances give thanks?
Are you mad?
Ever had the miseries, Paul—on top
of a tumor in the brain and an extra
hole in your head? Ever had a near-
lethal dose of Dilantin till you couldn't
walk for days? (Ever had three nurses
get you into your bath?)

This is the will of God? For you, maybe—
For me, if you don't mind, I prefer to think
someone else is back of this. Call it the Devil,
the vast impersonal forces of Nature,
call it chance, but do not call it GOD!

You say you know something about suffering, Paul?
"afflictions, hardships, calamities, beatings . . .
imprisonments, tumults, labors, watchings, hungering . . .
stoned and left for dead . . .

shipwrecked. . . ." Sure, I know,
those were terrible times for Christians . . .
especially for someone as brilliantly
provocative as you. . . .
But is it necessary, or helpful or even sane,
to "rejoice always" and give thanks in *all*
circumstances? What kind of theology
could see what happened to you or me as the
will of God? *Give me Jesus' God of love!*

What's that you say, Paul?
That one must wait until God is through
with a happening that looks evil to us?
That we cannot know consequences in advance?
That ours is to trust and wait . . .
That in God's perspective evil is often good
in disguise?
(May I observe that in my case the disguise
is perfect!)
That He makes the wrath of men to praise him?
Yes, that's somewhere in the Old Testament,
But is it a wish, a dream, whistling in the dark?
You say it is the Word, however it came. . . .

You're not backing down, Paul.
Listen, I know it worked out for you.
But you are part of that early church,
One of the founding fathers, an apostle.
You wrote Holy Writ, inspired
by God himself! There! I see
I've lost my case! It's no
longer you I'm arguing with.

I've often preached on your great text
in Romans 8: "In everything
God works for good with those who love him,
who are called according to his purpose."
A great text. I've used it at funerals.
You say I should now apply it
to my own condition?

That the Lord God Almighty is the original
alchemist, translating
the ashes and ignominy of our condition
into the pure gold of his kingdom
if only we trust him?

Furthermore, that what you have been saying
is simply the meaning of the cross,
the crucifixion of Jesus—that he said
it all very clearly in the Gospels?

Of course! I learned all that in
seminary! Basic theology! I've
preached it, taught it, explained it
ad nauseum. . . .
Now the time has come to live it?

You're saying the cross is for everyone,
and there hasn't been a loser yet?
Do you know what you're saying?
I guess you do. . . .

Yes, I hear it now: "Take up
your cross and follow me."
"He that loses his life for my sake
shall find it. . . ." It keeps on
happening?

OK, Jesus, Paul, Lou, God. . . .
I've got the message: I'm included.
But I warn you, I'll need a bit
of help. . . .

You'll be there with me?
Sure, I know you will! How else
could I have had this conversation
with you all?

                    E K

                    2/5/79

LET EVERY PAIN PRAISE GOD!

"Let every pain praise God!"
O you unsinkable Paulina Keck Klein,
O Mother o' mine—
How can I keep up with you,
all eighty-five years of you,
high blood pressure, glaucoma,
and what not!

Now you throw me another gem
from your thirty-below haven
in Bismarck, N.D.

It has to be original,
like from your pioneer
days on that Montana
homestead, with Dad away
riding the circuit of house churches
and preaching in schoolhouses.

Was it when sister Ruth was born,
and the midwife was miles away?
Was it the time you put carbide juice
from the gas lamp on your aching tooth
(at your stupid brother's suggestion)
and lost it?

Was it when Vi was born?
I remember that; Mrs. Frieh
was the midwife in Eureka, S.D.

Old Doc Brewster, the father
of organic chemistry at K.U.
used to tell of a woman in
childbirth before ether
or anesthesia. At intervals

she would say, "Whee! *That*
was a delicious one!"

But you, dear Mother, go
beyond mere savoring the inevitable.
You theologian, you!
"Let every pain praise God!"

Don't ever let anyone
shake your primitive faith.
It will get you there,
and me too!

E K

2/6/79

FAITH FANTASY

Sitting on a deck chair
in our pitch-pine grove in Maine,
    I hear the strawberries ripen. . . .

Lying on my back on the sand dune,
I see gulls wheel into the blue
    and hear the raspberries ripen.

Walking barefoot on the pine-needle carpet
of our yard, looking for new pitch-pine seedlings,
    I hear the burgeoning blueberries. . . .

Seeing the stars through the pines
and the moon booming up from the Atlantic,
    I smell the highbush cranberries!

Lord, what a harvest!
Clara, is that ice-cream freezer OK?
    We'll be getting company, you know!

      E K

      2/6/79

EXPERIENCE

Experience is the best teacher.
But when the subject is Death,
I prefer a substitute.

Three scenarios come to mind:

I.

The easiest way is when
the Angel of Death strikes suddenly
from a clear sky in bright daylight
as in a plane or auto crash.
No time to ask
> Did I leave my affairs in order?
> Did I leave enough?
> Will Clara manage?
> What will they say about me
> > when I'm gone?

II.

The worst way to go is the almost
imperceptible fading of strength,
coordination, memory, skills,
and attributes which make a person.

Cell by cell, fiber by fiber, muscle by
muscle, and nerve by nerve the body
fades to uselessness. . . .

Ashes to ashes, dust to dust. . . .
Every death is a reunion of the
estranged, the quiet homecoming of the
elements. Why should I be an
exception? Is it not good to
be part of the grand cycle?

And is one particular part so
much better than the others?

Then why do I struggle, withold
my consent?

"The natural history of this disease is
well known," says the doctor: "Death
within thirteen months from the first
diagnosis" (in my case, December 23).
I wink at Jan and say, "Merry Christmas!"

III.

Countdown
Shall we begin to cross days
off the calendar until Christmas
One more time . . .?
What I really don't want to see
is the Grim Reaper
all dressed up in a
Santa Claus suit!

E K

4/7/79

AFTERWORD

During the days of anxious waiting when we falsely believed that the attending doctors held the last word on Ernie's life, these poems became—for each of us who stood helplessly by—a new testament of hope, a window by which we could peer into our own uncertain futures. As Ernie has allowed us to enter into the depth and breadth of his own struggle to "say 'Yes' to death," he has ministered to us all and reminded us of the promise of the Lord of all life—"Lo, I am with you always."

Ernie's poems and his personal ministry have helped us discover that death is the author of the joy of living and in so doing has empowered us to face the abyss and shout with him: "Free at last! Thank God Almighty, I'm free at last!"

Richard Broholm

My DIALOGUE WITH DEATH

ERNST E KLEIN

Sarah OCT. 1 7 1993

236
CLASS   **ACC.**

_____
(LAST NAME OF AUTHOR)

MY DIALOGUE WITH DEATH
(BOOK TITLE)

FAIR LAWN BIBLE CHURCH
LIBRARY

STAMP LIBRARY OWNERSHIP

CODE 4386-03   BROADMAN SUPPLIES
CLS-3   MADE IN U.S.A.

BROADMAN